THE CONNECTICUT GUIDE TO CRIMINAL DEFENSE

By

Attorney Robert Fontaine, Attorney Brittany Paz, and Attorney Jim Ruane

Contributions by Emily Shouse

Edited by Jennifer Sanfilippo

 Printed in the United States of America
Different Middle Initial, LLC
ISBN: 978-1-7326411-5-0

Table of Contents

Introduction

Facing a criminal accusation in the state of Connecticut can be a daunting experience. You likely have a million questions running through your head at this time. Why was I charged? Will I have to go to jail? How can I defend myself?

At our law firm, we work with clients every day who have these questions and do not know where to turn. That is why we've created this book. We want to walk those facing criminal charges through the criminal justice system so that they have a better understanding of what is to come, what they face, and how they can protect their rights.

At Ruane Attorneys, we believe that everyone has the right to a fair trial and the right to understand the legal process that they face. We created this book to empower our clients and anyone else who is facing criminal proceedings in Connecticut. Throughout this book, we will cover issues such as:

- Bail and arraignment
- Miranda rights
- Motions in criminal cases
- Types of crimes, such as larceny, shoplifting, assault, firearm crimes, drug possession, and more

- Pleas, trials, and sentencing in the criminal justice system
- Diversionary programs
- Violation of probation

Becoming informed about the criminal justice process can answer many of your questions and ease your mind as you face this difficult experience. Of course, there is no substitute for an excellent criminal defense lawyer. We recommend that you use this book as an introduction to criminal defense in Connecticut, but we would also advise that you reach out to an attorney for help. You do not need to go through this experience alone. For more information, contact our office. We are happy to answer any additional questions that you have and help you through this experience.

About Us

Attorney Robert Fontaine

There are really only two things you need to know about me: I love winning, and I hate losing.

I don't come from a family full of lawyers, and I didn't always know that this is what I would do with my life, but whether I'm in a courtroom, on a ball field, or playing board games, those two things remain constant. I can't turn it off, and that competitiveness is ultimately what attracted me to practicing law. Every day in this field, I get to come into work and turn that attitude towards helping our clients achieve the best outcomes possible.

After I decided to pursue a career in the legal field, I received my J.D. from the University of Connecticut School of Law in 2015, and I joined the Ruane Attorneys staff in early 2019. The team-oriented environment and the culture has helped to foster the exact sort of competitive spirit that drew me to this sort of work originally. Having partners who are all seasoned and established litigators is a huge asset for the firm. It helps me focus my drive towards improving client outcomes.

Attorney Brittany Paz

Many people ask me why I would choose to be a criminal defense attorney. I suppose the answer has to do with one thing: fairness.

My mother always said that as a child I had a preoccupation with fairness. I would always tell her that this or that was unfair. As much as she tried to teach me that the world was unfair, I never really accepted the concept. I always strove to force more fairness in my everyday life.

My mother worked her entire career in law firms and so I grew up with the annual "take your daughter to work" day. The concept, which started in the 1990s, sought to raise awareness of feminism and promote women's advancement in the workplace. More importantly, it was meant to teach young girls that they truly could be anything they wanted. I took this seriously. I would go to my mother's law firm every year and sit in a conference room and look at a scene depicting a courtroom. One year, she asked me if I wanted to be a lawyer when I grew up. I replied, "No mommy, I want to be the judge!"

Ever since then, preoccupied with fairness, I strove to become an attorney. In law school, I quickly realized that the best place to achieve fairness, or justice, was in criminal court. I did a few internships and externships while in law school at the public defender's office and saw how the balance of power is distorted in the government's favor and hardworking, everyday people get steamrolled by prosecutors. I saw how the system sought to incarcerate people with mental illness and drug addiction rather than treat them. I witnessed the system separate families and insist on felony convictions with lifelong collateral consequences. Worst of all, I saw a system set up to only take heed of one side and put the weight of the State of Connecticut behind it. So, the choice was easy: to make the system more fair, become a criminal defense attorney.

More than a quarter of a century since first attending "take your daughter to work day," female criminal defense attorneys are still the exception rather than the rule. I noticed that I would wait to speak to the prosecutors and if there were ten attorneys in the room, only two were women. I always found this to be interesting, given that women offer their own unique perspective on cases and the needs of the client. While I found that I had to work a bit harder as I was routinely underestimated, I used that to my advantage and, undeterred, several years later I have established myself as one of the few female criminal defense attorneys in the state. I have achieved positive outcomes for clients on more than a hundred criminal cases ranging from motor vehicle tickets to murder. In 2018, 2019, and 2020, I was named National Trial Lawyers' "Top 40 Under 40" for criminal defense. I was also named a Super Lawyer 2020 Rising Star. I am proud to have crafted a niche in sex crimes, a field many criminal defense attorneys shy away from.

I know what it is like to be underestimated and unheard. I also understand the biting unfairness of the system.

Whether it be aggressive legal tactics, strong and effective negotiation, or whether you just need help or to be heard, we can work together to achieve the best possible outcome for your case.

Attorney Jim Ruane

For over 40 years, I have been a certified criminal trial specialist here in Connecticut. That makes me one of the few people in the field of law truly available to help you with your criminal case. In this book, I will do a deep dive into the basics of criminal defense and answer many of the questions I have gotten from clients and their family members over the last four decades.

I believe that no matter who you are, you have the right to a fair trial, and the presumption of innocence until proven guilty. This belief is at the core of my philosophy as a lawyer, and it is the reason why I started Ruane Attorneys with my son.

It might seem like a no brainer that lawyers will take this stance, but you will be surprised to find that this is not always true. Just like police officers and other members of the judicial system, lawyers develop prejudices against their clients and don't always listen to them. They put in minimal effort and move on to the next case, never stopping to think about the positive impact that they could have had on their clients, if only they tried a little harder.

After devoting most of my life to the profession of law, I have not become this kind of lawyer. I still strive to do my best for every single client.

I do this by staying active in the law community. I am one of only a handful of attorneys that are Certified Criminal Defense Specialists in the State of Connecticut. I am also a member of the National Board of Trial Advocacy, and a recipient of a Lifetime Achievement Award from the Connecticut Law Tribune.

I love the fact that every day, I have a chance to make a difference in someone else's life.

Chapter 1:

Covering the Basics

In this chapter, we will start with some basic terms that refer to things that occur even before an arrest, and that includes:

1. Reasonable and articulable suspicion
2. Probable cause
3. Beyond a reasonable doubt

Let's start with reasonable and articulable suspicion. Reasonable and articulable suspicion is the belief by a reasonable person that the suspect violated a law or regulation. This standard is objective; there is no specific equation or requirement as to what does or does not constitute reasonable suspicion. To meet this standard, law enforcement officers must be able to clearly articulate the facts they believe show a suspect has committed a crime. Essentially, they have to be able to point at a particular fact and say, "this is why I thought that." They can't just say, "I have a hunch," because a hunch is not articulable. Reasonable suspicion is a fact-specific inquiry on a case-by-case basis.

In Connecticut, our Appellate Court has defined what "reasonable and articulable suspicion" means. The official definition is: "What constitutes a reasonable and articulable suspicion depends on the totality of the circumstances...The determination of whether a specific set of circumstances provides a police officer with a reasonable and articulable suspicion of criminal activity is a question of fact for the trial court and is subject to limited appellate review." (Citations omitted.) State v. Anderson, 24 Conn. App. 438, cert. denied, 219 Conn. 903 (1991).

The police do not have to wait for a serious offense to stop your car. If they have reasonable articulable suspicion of any traffic violation – from speeding to driving with a broken tail light – they can lawfully pull you over to investigate. Some of the common factors that result in reasonable articulable suspicion include the following:

Driving the Wrong Way: Traveling in the wrong direction down a one-way street is against state law and many local ordinances. Police have the right to stop a driver heading the wrong way given the safety risks involved.

Speeding: Enforcing speeding laws is a major part of the job for most officers. If the police witness you driving even one mile over the speed limit, they have the authority to pull you over.

Running a Stop Sign: Traffic violations and car accidents are especially common at intersections. If you roll through a stop sign or fail to yield to a traffic light, an officer who sees you can stop you lawfully.

Mechanical Issues: There are quite a few regulations governing the maintenance of your vehicle. If your car lacks the necessary equipment required by law, a police officer can pull you over. This can include broken tail lights, missing license plates, or nonfunctioning headlights.

Now, sometimes police interaction occurs outside your car. In those situations, police conduct what is called a "Terry stop." If an officer reasonably believes that the detained individual might be armed and dangerous, the officer may undertake a pat down search to discover weapons. Terry v. Ohio, 392 U.S. 1 (1968); Trine, 236 Conn. at 223-224. See also State v. Days, 89 Conn. App. 789 (2005) - where officers conduct surveillance in an area known for narcotics activity and observed what appeared to be a drug transaction, they had reasonable and articulable suspicion to stop the suspect, even if they did not see drugs.

In Terry, the Supreme Court held that if a police officer believes that an individual has a weapon which poses a danger to the officer, the officer may stop that individual to search the individual for a weapon. The court held that to determine whether the police officer acted reasonably in the stop, a court should not look at whether the officer has a hunch, but rather, "to the specific reasonable inferences which he is entitled to draw from the facts in light of his experience." This could include knowledge that a particular area is considered "high crime," or knowledge that particular movements are consistent with hand-to-hand drug transactions. Therefore, the police are given a lot of chances to explain why it is that they stopped someone, and almost any reason could be sufficient. Even if the reason for the stop doesn't match the eventual charged crime, the stop will be sufficiently articulable.

Now, reasonable articulable suspicion is the first step on the staircase to reaching proof beyond all reasonable doubt. We use the staircase analogy because it is easy to understand that the prosecution must "climb the staircase" to reach their burden. The second step on the staircase is "probable cause."

The threshold of probable cause is familiar to a lot of people because it is often in movies or TV. It is important for you to know that such a term is used by police officers when they have arrested a defendant. Probable cause exists when the facts and circumstances within the knowledge of the officer and of which they have reasonable trustworthy information are sufficient in themselves to warrant a person of reasonable caution to believe a crime may have been committed. The evidence used to form probable cause may not necessarily be admissible in court, and the officers can rely on evidence like hearsay which would not be admissible at all in order to reach probable cause. At this point, they aren't looking for a guaranteed conviction, just enough to support an arrest decision.

Probable cause denotes a level of evidence which is the minimal level of proof required to justify an arrest of a defendant under our State and Federal Constitutions. Probable cause is not the equivalent of or interchangeable with the level of proof known as proof beyond a reasonable doubt.

Proof of probable cause does not mean a person is guilty. It only means there is enough evidence for an arrest, and it is the second step on the "staircase of guilt." If you have been arrested, it simply means that an officer believes they have probable cause that you committed an offense. A judge must make a finding of probable cause based on the officer's arrest warrant affidavit or police report before the case may proceed.

It is important to remember this fact when you have been charged - police *only* look at the bad stuff! They don't include possible defenses in their decision making for probable cause, and they only ever put bad stuff in the police reports and warrants. So, when you finally read what they wrote, it may make you out to be the devil, but that is not necessarily the case!

Now let's talk about the top step on the staircase - "reasonable doubt." Reasonable doubt is the standard used in criminal trials, and it is the highest level of proof.

The meaning of reasonable doubt derives from the emphasis of the word "reasonable." It is not a surmise, a guess, or mere conjecture. It is not a doubt raised by anyone simply for the sake of raising a doubt. It is such a doubt as, in serious affairs that concern a person, that person would heed; that is, such a doubt as would cause reasonable men and women to hesitate to act upon it in matters of importance. It is not hesitation springing from any feelings of pity or sympathy for the accused or any other person who might be affected by your decision. It is, in other words, a real doubt, an honest doubt, a doubt that has its foundation in the evidence or lack of evidence. It is doubt that is honestly entertained and is reasonable in light of the evidence, after a fair comparison and careful examination of the entire evidence.

To put it another way - proof beyond a reasonable doubt is proof that leaves a person firmly convinced of the defendant's guilt. There are very few things in the world that we know with absolute certainty. In criminal law cases, the law does not require proof that overcomes every possible doubt. If, based on consideration of the evidence, a person is firmly convinced that the defendant is guilty of the crime charged, they should find the defendant guilty. If, on the other hand, based on the evidence or lack of evidence, they have a reasonable doubt as to the defendant's guilt, they must give the defendant the benefit of that doubt and find them not guilty.

As you can see, proof beyond all reasonable doubt is a very high standard, and rightfully so, because we don't want anyone convicted based on anything less than this level of certainty.

Chapter 2:

Bail and Arraignment

When a person is arrested by the police, bail will be set for the case. Bail is a financial incentive to return to court. It is an amount of money set by the judge or the police. The point of bail is both to protect the community and make sure that a person comes to their scheduled court dates to answer the charges, until the case is resolved.

In the case of an on-site arrest, the police will set bail when you are arrested for a crime. If a warrant is submitted to the court, a judge will set the bond in the arrest warrant, once it is signed. If you are able to post the full bail amount in cash, then you will be released from jail and given a court date to appear in the future. When the case ends, you can get a full refund of the cash that you posted to the court.

If you aren't able to post bail by yourself, then you can contact a bail bondsman, who will post bail on your behalf. The bail bond is like an insurance policy. You pay a non-refundable premium, and the bail bondsman agrees, in writing, to cover the bail amount if you fail to appear for one of the court dates. Bondsmen typically charge between 7% and 10% of the bail amount as the premium for the bail bond. The bail bondsman will give a written bail bond to the police and then the police will release you.

For example, if the police set a $5,000 bail for a case, the defendant will have to pay the bail bondsman $500. You do not get that money back at the end of the case. It becomes the bondsman's fee. If you had paid the entire $5,000 in cash by yourself, then you could get a full refund at the end of the case. But most people don't have that amount of cash on hand, so many of our clients use a bail bondsman. Connecticut law allows you to post 10% of your bail up to $20,000. It is a way to get out and not incur the cost of a bondsman, but you either need to post it in cash, or have someone post it in cash for you.

Your first court date after your arrest will be the arraignment. This is a very significant court date where several critical things will happen. If you are still being held in police custody at this time, the judge will review the amount of bail set by the police. The judge can set a new amount of bail bond so that you can be released. If you were unable to post bond, and are still in jail, you will be interviewed by special court staff called Bail Commissioners. These individuals then make recommendations to the judge about the amount of bail, based on their interview. Also, the judge will review the arrest reports to ensure that the police had probable cause for the arrest.

The judge has the right to raise or lower the amount of bail at a court date. This is why, depending on the circumstances of the bond that is set, it may be wise to bond out from the police station, or it may be wise to wait and see if the court lowers the bond amount. Only a lawyer who has worked with criminal cases can give you good advice to assist with your situation. Also, the judge has the right to add non-financial conditions as further conditions of release. These non-financial release conditions can include protective orders in domestic cases, restrictions on possession of firearms, counseling and treatment, substance abuse testing and treatment, GPS monitoring, travel restrictions, and more. If you fail to obey any of these release conditions, you will be re-arrested and you will be charged with the additional crime of violation of conditions of release, a Class A misdemeanor.

If you miss your court date, the judge can "call the bond" and order a re-arrest by placing an additional bond on you. If you posted cash bail, it will be forfeited to the court. Worse, if a bail bondsman posted your bond, they will hire a bounty hunter to find you and bring you back to court. You will also be charged with Failure to Appear, which may be a misdemeanor or a felony depending on your underlying charges. You should avoid this situation and always make sure to appear at your scheduled court dates.

Chapter 3:

Miranda Rights

On June 13, 1966, the outcome of Miranda v. Arizona, 384 U.S. 436 (1966) provided that suspects have to be informed of their constitutional rights required by the Fifth and Sixth Amendments when they are placed under arrest. This decision was based on a case in which a defendant, Ernesto Miranda, was accused of robbery, kidnapping, and rape. During a police interrogation, he confessed to the crimes and was convicted.

The conviction was overturned due to allegedly intimidating police interrogation methods. After a retrial that included witnesses and other evidence, Miranda was again convicted. His trial was, however, then assured of being fair, and the original conviction was reasonably upheld without question.

Prior to the institution of the *Miranda* Warning, confessions only had to be voluntary on the part of the suspect. This created a difficult situation for police, who were then often faced with evidence at trial that the person was not of sound mind or were under circumstantial duress when they gave their confession.

The *Miranda* Warning protects an individual's rights by explaining their options clearly. It upholds police authority when they properly read the *Miranda* Warning and get a clear, intelligent answer that the suspect understands their rights as they have been explained and are waiving them by continuing to give a statement to the police. Principally, *Miranda* is a warning and a waiver of constitutional rights. The *Miranda* Warning is a legal requirement throughout the United States, though no right is absolute.

Now that you understand what the *Miranda* Rights are and where they came from, let's talk about why they don't matter most of the time. There are basically two types of crimes. First are general intent crimes, and second, there are specific intent crimes.

For general intent crimes, the only thing that really matters is that the crime happened and that the defendant did it. For example, in a DUI case, the prosecutor doesn't have to prove that you intended to drive drunk, they only have to prove that you a) were driving, and b) that you were doing so over the legal limit of blood alcohol content. Similarly, if you are charged with breach of peace causing another person annoyance or alarm, it doesn't matter if you intended to cause that result, only that you did, in fact, act, which caused that result. Those are general intent crimes. Your mental state is irrelevant for the crime to be charged.

Because your mental state is not an issue in these cases, the police don't have to prove that you *intentionally* committed an act. They just have to get enough evidence to arrest you with probable cause for the act itself. In this case, the police still must give *Miranda* Warnings if the person is under arrest and being interrogated. This is another reason why whenever you interact with police you should simply be quiet. You can't talk your way out of an arrest, but you sure can talk yourself into more charges.

To be clear, the requirements for *Miranda* are 1) that the person is in custody and 2) the person is being interrogated. There are certain requirements for the *Miranda* Warning. If a person chooses to remain silent after *Miranda* Warnings, the police can still ask the suspect his or her name and address but the suspect does not need to answer substantive questions. Because of this reason, police generally do not have the need to interrogate the person. The *Miranda* Warning is only required when the police intend to interrogate the person while that person is in custody. Only when the police determine that the person is a suspect that they will interrogate does the questioning become custodial and *Miranda* Warnings must be given.

Now, for other crimes, such as intentional murder, it *does* matter what the person was thinking at the time the crime was committed. This is an example of a specific intent crime. The police want to interrogate suspects in these cases to find out more about what their involvement was in the crime and what their state of mind was at the time. They can't be mind readers, so instead, they are allowed to question you after explanation and waiver of your *Miranda*

Rights, however, the suspect being questioned may choose to remain silent and ask for a lawyer.

One of the big issues we see as criminal defense lawyers is that too often, people start talking when dealing with the police, and talk themselves into a case. Many times, suspects in question will remain silent, invoking that right until they decide to talk and answer questions. They don't know that if they don't offer up any information, the police may not have enough evidence to arrest them. You cannot be forced to speak to the police.

Remember, handcuffs are silver, and silence is golden. Gold outranks silver, so keep your mouth shut.

Chapter 4:

Motions in Criminal Cases

Whenever you see lawyers in the media, they are often seen filing paperwork on behalf of their clients. This is usually done in the form of a motion. A motion is a request for the court to take action in a case. For the most part, in criminal cases we see two types of motions: the Motion to Dismiss, and the Motion to Suppress. We'll talk more about these types of motions in this chapter.

A Motion to Dismiss is exactly what it sounds like. It is a request that the judge dismiss the charges against someone because of a legal defect in the case. Bases for Motions to Dismiss may include a jurisdiction issue, which is a claim that the case should be dismissed because it is brought in the wrong court. Or, they may claim that the state can't show probable cause for a case to a neutral judge. In other situations, for example after the completion of a diversionary program, a Motion to Dismiss will be made by the defense because the client is entitled to a dismissal of the charges by operation of law.

A Motion to Suppress usually is filed when the police or prosecution may have done something illegal to obtain evidence. When they undertake an illegal act, they should not get the benefit of using the evidence against you. So this is when a lawyer would file a Motion to Suppress citing your Fourth and Fifth Amendment rights. It is important to note that winning Motions to Suppress do not guarantee that a case will be dismissed. It simply means that the state cannot use that piece of evidence against you at your trial. If there is other evidence from which a jury may infer guilt beyond a reasonable doubt, a case may still proceed.

Now let's talk about searches. The Fourth Amendment to the United States Constitution, and Article 1 subsection 7 of the Connecticut Constitution, prohibit unreasonable searches and seizures. Article 1 subsection 7 of Connecticut's Constitution mirrors the Fourth Amendment of the United States Constitution and reads as follows:

"The people shall be secure in their persons, houses, papers and effects from unreasonable searches or seizures; and no warrant to search any place, or to seize any person or things, shall issue without describing them as nearly as may be, nor without probable cause supported by oath or affirmation."

The touchstone of Fourth Amendment analysis is whether a person has a, "'constitutionally protected reasonable expectation of privacy.'" Katz v. United States, 389 U.S. 347, 360 (1967). Where a defendant can show an actual objective expectation of privacy in the place searched (or object seized) and that this objective expectation of privacy is one that society is prepared to recognize as reasonable, the government must have a warrant supported by probable cause before effecting the search, unless it fits some other recognized exception to the warrant requirement. Conversely, without a reasonable expectation of privacy, a search performed by government officials or a public employer will not violate the Fourth Amendment, regardless of the search's nature and scope.

This provision is significant to a criminal defendant because evidence that is "unreasonably" seized may be inadmissible in the case against them. As nearly every prosecution involving drugs involves the admission of those drugs into evidence, this constitutional protection and related "exclusionary rule" is of paramount importance to the defendant facing drug charges because, as a practical matter, if the introduction of narcotics can be prevented by establishing the illegality of the seizure or search which turned up evidence, the prosecution will be defeated.

The initial burden of going forward on a pretrial Motion to Suppress is on the defendant, but the burden of proof is on the state for most of the issues governing whether evidence obtained by the state should be suppressed. The Connecticut Practice Book allows the defendant to file a Motion to Suppress potential testimony or other evidence, arguing for suppression required under the Constitution or laws of the United States or the state of Connecticut. Under the Practice Book and section 54-33f of the Connecticut General Statutes, the defendant can also file a Motion to Suppress evidence, obtained without a warrant, where a warrant was required.

EXCEPTIONS TO THE WARRANT REQUIREMENT

Search Incident to Arrest

When officers have probable cause to make an arrest, they can lawfully search the person pursuant to a search warrant. This is to ensure that there are no dangerous items on your person while you are being taken into custody as well as to inventory the items in your possession for return later.

The "Open Handed Pat Down"

When individuals are stopped for suspected narcotics activity, it is reasonable for officers to conclude that the subjects might be armed and dangerous, because narcotics activity is the type of activity that can result in sudden violence. When an individual is lawfully detained pursuant to a Terry stop, officers may conduct an "open-handed pat down" to check for weapons or contraband. Officers do not need to be positive that a suspect has a weapon to conduct a lawful pat down; they are allowed to make reasonable inferences based on the surrounding circumstances and their prior experiences.

Furthermore, there is a well-established connection between drugs and firearms. Under Terry, an officer is allowed to conduct an open-handed pat down of the suspect to check for weapons. It does not become a search until the officer has to manipulate the object to determine what it is. Only then have they exceeded the lawful scope of a Terry pat down. Minnesota v. Dickerson, 508 U.S. 366 (1993); Trine 37 Conn. App. at 233. If, however, they immediately recognize the object as a weapon or contraband without manipulation, that's considered the "plain feel" doctrine and is a lawful search and seizure if they remove it from the defendant's person.

Inventory Search

When a police officer has made a lawful custodial arrest of the occupants of an automobile they may, as a contemporaneous incident of that arrest, search the passenger compartment of the vehicle. This is called an inventory search. Our Appellate Court in State v. Whealton, 108 Conn. App. 172 (2008) has further explained the inventory search of a car: "[the inventory search is] a well-defined exception to the warrant requirement...In the performance of their community care-taking functions, the police are frequently obliged to take automobiles into their custody...A standardized procedure for making a list or inventory as soon as reasonable after reaching the station house not only deters false claims but also inhibits theft or careless handling of articles taken from the arrested person." Whealton, 108 Conn. App. at 179.

The officer may also examine the contents of any container found within the passenger compartment and such "container" (i.e. an object capable of holding another object) may be searched whether it is open or closed. New York v. Belton, 453 U.S. 454 (1981); State v. Delossantos, 211

Conn. 258 (1989). Furthermore, when the hatchback area of the car can be reached from the interior, passenger area, it can also be searched incident to arrest. Delossantos, 211 Conn. at 257.

Plain View

If the police are in a lawful position to view an item that is immediately recognizable as a weapon or contraband, that item may be seized without a warrant. Coolidge v. New Hampshire, 91 S.Ct. 2022, 2039 (1971). For example, if the police conduct a lawful motor vehicle stop, and the police come up to your driver's side window and may see, in plain view, a handgun in your center console, the officer may then take you out of the vehicle, conduct a pat down search for additional weapons, and seize the weapon if the investigation determines that your possession of the weapon is unlawful.

Automobile Exception

Police officers may conduct a search of the entire automobile, including the truck and containers in the car, if they have probable cause to believe that contraband can be found in the car. Coolidge, 91 S.Ct. at 2039. This is commonly known as the automobile exception. The justification for the automobile exception is twofold: (1) the inherent mobility of an automobile creates exigent circumstances (i.e. a person can drive away quickly and evidence may be destroyed); and (2) the expectation of privacy with respect to one's automobile is significantly less than that relating to one's home or office. State v. Wilson, 111 Conn. App. 614 (2008).

Probable cause to search exists if, "(1) there is probable cause to believe that the particular items sought to be seized are connected with criminal activity or will assist in a particular apprehension or conviction and (2) there is probable cause to believe that the items sought to be seized will be found in the place to be searched." Wilson at 624. If an officer has probable cause, they can also search the trunk of the automobile. State v. Kuskowski, 200 Conn. 82 (1986).

Oftentimes, probable cause is obtained by use of a canine who is trained to detect either drugs or firearms. If the canine "alerts," that will provide probable cause to search the vehicle. Also, where a police officer represents in their report that they, "smelled the odor of marijuana," the court will find probable cause for a further search of the automobile for drugs.

Exigent Circumstances

The home is the most protected space recognized by law. In order to search your home, the police traditionally need a warrant supported by probable cause and the warrant must be signed by a neutral and detached magistrate (if there are no exigent circumstances such as a fleeing felon). There are some notable exceptions, including exigent circumstances. See Kentucky v. King, 131 S. Ct. 1849, 1852 (2011). An exigent circumstance may be present where the police receive a phone call of an assault in progress in a residence and arrive to hear screaming on the other side of the door. Police may then be warranted in entering the home despite the lack of a warrant.

Protective Sweep

If the officers think someone else is in the house that poses a danger, they can also look for weapons in the areas immediately adjoining where the defendant is arrested, even if not authorized by the warrant. Maryland v. Buie, 110 S.Ct. 1093, 1098-99 (1990). In State v. Williams, 110 Conn. App. 329 (2008), the Connecticut Appellate Court held that where officers possess a reasonable belief based on specific and articulable facts that areas in the house to be swept harbor an individual posing a danger to those at the arrest scene, the officers may engage in a limited search for such individual. The search is limited to those areas where an individual can be found (i.e. cannot be in a drawer).

They can also search for weapons in areas immediately adjoining where the defendant is arrested, even if they are already handcuffed. This exception is important because if the officer is lawfully present, anything they can observe in plain view which is immediately recognizable as contraband (i.e. drugs or weapons) can be seized lawfully.

Also, there is no "good faith exception" to the warrant requirement in Connecticut. Unlike federal courts, the Connecticut state constitution does not allow for a good faith exception to the warrant requirement. If a warrant is facially defective, the evidence cannot be admitted under the "good faith" exception. Even so, if there was another, lawful way that the government could have obtained this evidence, it may still be admissible. This is called the "inevitable discovery" doctrine. Nix v. U.S., 467 U.S. 431 (1984).

Police officers may also conduct an investigatory frisk of the passengers in an automobile if they believe that a passenger in the automobile possesses a weapon. When a reasonable and articulable suspicion exists, the detaining officer may conduct an investigative stop of the suspect to confirm or to dispel their suspicions. Terry v. Ohio, 392 U.S. 1 (1968); State v. Federici, 179 Conn. 46 (1979); State v. Acklin, 171 Conn. 105 (1976). During a "Terry stop," an officer may search the automobile's passenger compartment for weapons, limited to areas where the weapon might be hidden, if he or she reasonably believes the suspect is potentially dangerous. Michigan v. Long, 463 U.S. 1032 (1983).

The law on searches is complicated and challenging even to lawyers with decades of experience. Every case that has a suppression issue should be investigated by a criminal defense lawyer to make sure you get the best defense.

Chapter 5:

Larceny & Shoplifting Crimes

Larceny is a common crime, usually committed out of necessity or opportunity. A person commits larceny when, with intent to deprive another of property or to appropriate the same to themselves or a third person, they wrongfully take, obtain, or withhold such property from an owner. The person accused of larceny has to have intended to deprive someone else of property for the charge to stick. This is the difference between defining something as theft and defining it as "borrowing" or "forgetting to return" property. Also, the state will have to prove that you intended to steal and keep property if they are going to convict you of this crime. Alternatively, you can try to prove that you did not have this intention when building your defense.

Larceny can take many forms, including:

- Embezzlement
- Obtaining property by false pretenses
- Obtaining property by false promise
- Acquiring property lost, mislaid, or delivered by mistake
- Extortion
- Defrauding of the public community

- Theft of services
- Receiving stolen property
- Shoplifting
- Conversion of a motor vehicle
- Obtaining property through fraudulent use of an ATM
- Library theft
- Conversion of leased property
- Failing to pay prevailing rate of wages
- Theft of utility service
- Airbag fraud
- Theft of motor fuel

We get a lot of questions about larceny charges every year, and these are the most common.

What is the First Step I Should Take After Getting Charged With Larceny?

The very first thing that you should do if you are charged with larceny is to contact a criminal defense lawyer. You should not give statements to the police without a lawyer present, even if you believe the charge is just a misunderstanding. A lawyer can help you navigate police questioning and build a case to defend yourself to ensure that you get a proper defense in court.

If I Borrowed Property and Didn't Return It, Can I Face Larceny Charges?

A major factor in a larceny or theft charge is intent. Therefore, the answer to this question depends on your particular situation. If you borrowed a friend or neighbor's property and genuinely forgot to return it, a larceny charge probably won't stick. However, if you borrowed property and didn't return it on purpose, you could face conviction for larceny. The state is allowed to present to the jury reasonable inferences from behavior, because, absent a confession, jurors cannot read minds. Many facts and circumstances may lead to a reasonable inference that the failure to return an item was not a mistake. Such circumstances may include the failure to return it despite numerous requests, and a showing of ways by which the complainant and police attempted to contact you about the item.

If I Borrowed Property But Later Returned It, Can I Face a Larceny Charge?

Again, this will depend on the situation that you find yourself in. If you borrowed property with the knowledge of the property's owner and returned it by a time that you and the owner previously agreed on, they probably won't press charges. However, if you only return the property under the threat of charges, but you did not intend to return it, you could face a larceny charge.

If I Steal Something as a Joke, Can I Face Larceny Charges?

As we have mentioned, larceny occurs when one person deliberately intends to permanently deprive an owner of their property. If you take something as a practical joke, your lawyer might argue that you were not trying to deprive the owner of the property. This situation, like many others, will depend on the circumstances of your case, the facts presented in court, and the determination of a judge or jury. Some judges or juries might find it hard to believe that even if you stole something as a joke, that you genuinely did not realize that taking it would deprive the owner of it. If this is the case, you could get convicted of larceny.

Can a Minor Face Larceny Charges?

Juveniles can indeed face larceny charges. However, in many cases, they face less severe punishments than adults.

What Are the Degrees of Larceny?

Under the statutory scheme in Connecticut, the grade of the offense of larceny ranges from larceny in the first degree, to larceny in the sixth degree. You might wonder how larceny is charged for these different degrees. These grades generally depend on the value of the property stolen. So, your charge will depend on what you are accused of. We can break it down as follows:

Degree of Larceny	Amount of Property Involved	Classification
First Degree	Over $20,000	Class B Felony
Second Degree	Over $10,000	Class C Felony
Third Degree	Over $2,000	Class D Felony
Fourth Degree	Over $1,000	Class A Misdemeanor
Fifth Degree	Over $500	Class B Misdemeanor
Sixth Degree	$500 or less	Class C Misdemeanor

Shoplifting is another common form of larceny and usually falls in the lower levels of larceny. Shoplifting is when someone steals something from a retail establishment or a market. Shoplifting is a common crime of opportunity oftentimes committed by teenagers. If you have been charged with shoplifting, perhaps there are some explanations for your actions that can mitigate the charge and get you the right result since it is so out-of-character. We are trained in seeking these out and advocating for you with them. Here are a few common questions that we get about shoplifting:

Can a Store Detain Me If They Suspect Me of Shoplifting? Isn't That Kidnapping?

No, it is not kidnapping. The store can detain you to allow the police to arrive. Many times, people find themselves in the store manager's office and try to talk their way out of the situation - but successfully talking your way out of shoplifting rarely happens. If a store has called the police, the best advice is to remain silent, so as to not make the situation worse.

I Was Arrested For Shoplifting and Got a Letter From the Store Saying I Owe Them Money - Should I Pay It? And Does That Make the Case Go Away?

No, you should not pay it because it is an admission by you that you indeed shoplifted at the store. In addition, paying the store does not make any potential criminal charge go away. Stores usually have letters sent out to try to gain money from shoplifters, but paying it does not make the charges go away. If you get this letter, you should bring it to your attorney right away.

Chapter 6:

Assault Crimes

Facing an assault charge can greatly disrupt your life and interfere with your everyday routine. You might be facing issues such as posting bail, a restraining order, or other issues that can alter your life. In addition, you have to start thinking about how you will build your defense and prevent an assault conviction. All of this can seem overwhelming and frustrating. But, the good news is that you don't have to go through it alone. By hiring a criminal defense attorney who has worked with assault cases before, you can rest assured that everything possible to protect your rights will happen.

First off - let's talk about some important things to know:

- You can be liable for the cost of all injuries in a criminal matter, and may also be liable for injuries in a civil matter.
- There is no bright line rule as to what a serious physical injury or what a physical injury is in the state of Connecticut.
- Purely emotional trauma does not constitute serious physical injury for purposes of the assault statute.

- The focus of a prosecution under reckless assault is not based upon the resulting injuries to the victim, but is based upon the actions of the accused.

If you are charged with assault in Connecticut, it is important to know that there are three major types, including assault in the first, second, and third degree.

Of the three, assault in the third degree is the least serious, as it is classified as a Class A misdemeanor, and the other types of assault are felonies. Regardless, third degree assault carries penalties of up to $2,000 in fines and up to a year in prison. You can be charged with third degree assault if:

- You cause physical injury to someone with intent to hurt them;
- You recklessly cause serious injury to someone; or
- With criminal negligence, you cause injury with a weapon.

Second degree assault is considered a felony, but it is a Class D or C felony, meaning it is less serious than first degree assault. The penalties for second degree assault include a fine of up to $5,000 and a 1-5 year prison sentence. You will be charged with second degree assault if you:

- Cause serious physical harm with intent;
- Use a deadly weapon (other than a firearm) with the intent to cause serious physical injury and do so;

- Recklessly cause serious physical harm by use of a deadly weapon;
- Drug someone;
- Kick or otherwise strike a person in the head with the intent to cause unconsciousness and doing so; or
- Kick or otherwise strike a person in a lying position with the intent to cause serious physical harm.

First degree assault is considered the most serious type of assault. It is classified as a Class B felony and the penalties can be as high as a $15,000 fine and 20 years in prison. Please note that in Connecticut, if you are convicted of certain kinds of first degree assault, you face a mandatory minimum of five years in prison. First degree assault carries such serious penalties because it involves:

- Serious physical injury caused by a gun or other weapon with intent;
- Intent to cause serious disfigurement;
- Reckless behavior that can result in death, causing serious physical injury;
- Serious physical injury while aided by two or more persons present; or
- Physical injury by use of a firearm with intent.

The most common assault-type behaviors charged overall are three misdemeanors: Breach of Peace, Threatening, and Disorderly Conduct. Every year thousands of people are charged with these offenses.

There are a number of crimes that fall into the assault category in Connecticut. Oftentimes, assault charges are brought in connection with domestic violence cases, but you don't have to know the person to be charged with assault. We have successfully represented people who have been the victim of assault who are charged when the police fail to investigate and charge everyone at a fight as committing the offense.

Certain segments of our population that are at risk of harm have special assault protections. Those people, like the elderly, who are protected with assault on them in the first, second and third degree, have the most protections. Blind, disabled, or pregnant people also have special protections in the law, because of their heightened chance of being victims of assault-type behavior.

Another category of people who have been given special protection in the assault laws are first responders and law enforcement. If you are charged with assault on a police officer, corrections officer or, fire or EMS worker, you face enhanced penalties simply because of their job.

As many assault crimes are specific intent offenses, one such defense to assault of a protected person includes proving that you did not know that the victim had a disability or pregnancy. If you didn't know about these special circumstances and you can prove this in court, the state attorney may be willing to reduce the charge to a lower level assault. This defense can be difficult to prove in court, so it is in your best interest to hire a criminal defense lawyer who can assist you with building your defense.

Another common defense for assault is acting in self-defense. If you feel that you did not instigate the incident that you were involved in, or if you were provoked into action because you felt threatened, you can use self-defense as a legitimate excuse for your actions. To find out if self-defense is a viable defense in your situation, you should contact a criminal defense lawyer. A lawyer will be able to determine the facts of your case and how a judge or jury will view them.

Chapter 7:

Firearm Crimes

The Second Amendment protects the rights of American citizens to keep and bear arms. However, in exercising those rights you must still abide by any applicable state laws regulating the lawful ownership and use of firearms.

Connecticut has some of the most complex and strict laws regarding gun ownership in the country, making the assistance of an attorney very helpful.

In addition, recent legislation has heightened the requirements and obligations of gun owners in the state of Connecticut. The violation of any of the laws relating to lawful gun ownership can have serious consequences.

One of the most common firearm charges is Carrying Pistol Without a Permit (Conn. Gen. Stat. § 29-35(a)). This is a Class D felony that carries a one year mandatory minimum unless the court determines mitigating circumstances. A possible defense to this crime is if you had possession of the gun in your home or within the home's curtilage. Any firearm found in possession of a person while in violation of the statute shall be forfeited.

Failure to Carry Pistol Permit (Conn. Gen. Stat. § 29-35(b)) is another firearms offense. This is an infraction and carries a fine of $35. Conn. Gen. Stat. § 29-37(c).

Illegal Carry of Firearm While Under the Influence of Drugs or Alcohol (Conn. Gen. Stat. § 53-206d(a)) is a Class B misdemeanor. The State can charge this offense if your blood alcohol content (BAC) is .08 or higher.

Illegal Possession of Weapon in Motor Vehicle (Conn. Gen. Stat. § 29-38) includes carrying a firearm when a proper permit has not been issued. It is a Class D felony.

Violating Pistol Permit Requirements (Conn. Gen. Stat. § 29-28) is a Class E felony relating to the sale of firearms and any firearm found in possession of a person while in violation of the statute shall be forfeited. Conn. Gen. Stat. § 29-37(a).

Violating Pistol Permit Requirements - Unauthorized Premises (Conn. Gen. Stat. § 29-28(e)) is a Class E felony and relates to carrying a firearm, whether or not permitted, on premises where firearms are prohibited, such as schools. Any firearm found in possession of a person while in violation of the statute shall be forfeited. Conn. Gen. Stat. § 29-37(a).

In 2013, legislation banning assault weapons was passed in Connecticut following the Sandy Hook school shooting, making the possession of any weapon that meets the legal definition of an assault weapon a felony offense. An assault weapon includes any selective-fire firearm that is fully automatic, semi-automatic, or can burst fire, semi-automatic centerfire rifles, pistols, shotguns that meet certain features regarding the magazine, grip, length, amount of rounds it can fire, etc.

In addition, magazines holding more than 10 rounds may no longer be lawfully sold, purchased, or imported into the State. Doing so is a Class D felony. Possession of a high capacity magazine obtained after the ban is also a Class D felony; however, possession of a magazine that was obtained before the ban but not registered is a first time infraction, but a felony for subsequent violations. Conn. Gen. Stat. § 53-202w.

While the possession of high-capacity magazines purchased prior to the ban is not unlawful, these magazines must be registered and you can no longer register them. They were required to be registered prior to the law's effective date of January 1, 2014. If they were not registered prior to that date and there is no legitimate reason for the delay, you may need to surrender possession or be guilty of a felony. Even if registered, the high capacity magazine may only be possessed at the person's residence or business, a licensed shooting range, or for transportation between those places. A violation of this provision is a Class C misdemeanor according to Conn. Gen. Stat. § 53-202x(g).

While most states require a prospective purchaser to pass a background check before buying a handgun, Connecticut requires a national criminal background check for the sale of long guns as well. Although most states do not regulate the sale of long guns, in Connecticut these purchases are documented in the same way as the lawful transfer and purchase of handguns. Guns may not be loaded when transfers are made.

Connecticut does not recognize out-of-state carry licenses or permits from any state. In order to carry a firearm lawfully in Connecticut, you must apply for a Connecticut State Permit to Carry Pistols and Revolvers. However, before obtaining a State Permit, you must first obtain a "local" or "temporary" permit by filing an application with your town's local police chief. If your request for a temporary permit is approved, a copy of your application will be forwarded to the Commissioner of Emergency Services and Public Protection for review. Once received, the Commissioner will have eight weeks to approve or deny your application for a Connecticut State Permit to Carry Pistols and Revolvers.

A bona fide United States resident that does not reside in Connecticut, but who has a permit or license to carry by the authority of another state, may apply directly to the Commissioner of Emergency Services and Public Protection for a non-resident Connecticut State Permit to Carry Pistols and Revolvers. Conn. Gen. Stat. §§ 29-28; 29-28a.

Nonresidents permitted to possess and carry handguns in their home state may transport handguns in Connecticut without a Connecticut permit for the purpose of (1) participating in competitions, (2) participating in formal handgun training at a locally approved or permitted firing range or training facility, (3) taking the firearm for repair, or

(4) attending meetings or exhibitions of organized gun collectors.

Non-residents may transport handguns without a Connecticut permit through Connecticut for lawful purposes in accordance with federal law if they are not otherwise prohibited from shipping, transporting, receiving, or possessing guns and are transporting them between states where they can legally possess and carry them. Conn. Gen. Stat. §§ 29-28; 29-28a; 29-30; 29-38d.

Connecticut's carry statute covers pistols and revolvers exclusively. A "pistol" or "revolver" is defined as any firearm with a barrel less than twelve inches long. Connecticut requires special permits for purchasing firearms and ammunition. In order to purchase a handgun in Connecticut, you must be a Connecticut resident, at least 21 years of age, and possess either (1) a valid Permit to Carry Pistols or Revolvers or (2) a valid Eligibility Certificate to Purchase Pistols or Revolvers. An Eligibility Certificate to Purchase Pistols or Revolvers entitles the holder to purchase a firearm and transport the same to their residence or place of business but does not entitle the holder to carry a pistol or revolver on their person.

Likewise, in order to purchase a long gun in Connecticut, you must be at least 18 years of age, and possess either (1) a valid Permit to Carry Pistols or Revolvers, (2) a valid Eligibility to Purchase Pistols or Revolvers, or (3) a valid Eligibility Certificate to Purchase Long Guns. If the long gun is a semi-automatic centerfire rifle that has or accepts a magazine with a capacity of more than five rounds, the purchaser must be at least 21 years of age. To purchase ammunition in Connecticut, you must be at least 18 years of age, and possess either (1) a valid Permit to Carry Pistols or Revolvers, (2) a valid Eligibility to Purchase Pistols or Revolvers, (3) a valid Eligibility Certificate to Purchase Long Guns, or (4) a valid Ammunition Certificate and a valid form of government-issued identification.

Connecticut law requires individuals who have been convicted of any offense involving the use or threatened use of a deadly weapon to register with the Connecticut Department of Emergency Services and Public Protection (DESPP) for a period of five years after serving their sentence. Registrants are required to check in with local law enforcement each year. Connecticut's deadly weapon offender registry is the first statewide weapons offender registry of its kind.

When purchasing a firearm, you will be required to fill out Form 4473, also referred to as the Firearms Transaction Record. If a person wants to purchase a firearm from a Federal Firearm License (FFL) holder, their form has to be filled out. For example, if you want to purchase a gun or another firearm from a gun shop, you need to provide this form.

On Form 4473, you need to provide some personal information. This includes information such as:

- Your name
- Your address

- Your date of birth
- National Instant Criminal Background Check System (NICS) transaction number
- Government issued photo identification
- A short statement that you are eligible to buy firearms according to federal law
- You also need to fill out the make, model, or serial number of the firearm you wish to purchase

The firearm dealer will copy all of your information from Form 4473 into a book called the Acquisition and Disposition Log. If the Bureau of Alcohol, Tobacco, Firearms, and Explosives (ATF) asks for a copy of your Form 4473 during a criminal investigation, they are required to hand it over. Dealers are also required to report certain kinds of sales to ATF. For example, any sale of two or more handguns within a five day period to one person must be reported. The dealer is required to keep this information on file for at least twenty years. When the dealer retires from the firearm business, they have to surrender their Acquisition and Disposition Log to the ATF.

If you want to buy a firearm from a person who is not a licensed dealer, most states won't require that you fill out Form 4473. However, if you are purchasing a handgun from a private individual, Form 4473 must be filled out before the sale can take place.

If you purposefully lie on your Form 4473, you are subject to a felony. The consequences are as much as five years in prison and a fine. This is the case even if NICS denies the transaction. Prosecution of this crime is common in Connecticut by the United States' Attorney's office in federal court, and it is not something that you should take a chance with. Avoid lying on your Form 4473 at all costs. Don't use the lie and try method - it is a very easy crime to prove!

As you can see, Connecticut has a lot of laws and regulations around guns and firearms, and if you have been charged with one, it is important to get a gun lawyer fighting your case for you.

Chapter 8:

Drug Crimes

With the recent news of marijuana decriminalization and recreational use in other parts of the country, it would make sense that drug crimes are not as serious anymore, but that is not true.

Drug possession and sales are still prosecuted every day in Connecticut and taken very seriously by the prosecutors across the state. Many of them do not agree with the relaxation of the laws on marijuana and possession of marijuana still forms a basis to support probable cause for automobile searches.

The most common drug crimes are "possession of a controlled substance" and "illegal distribution/sale of a controlled substance." "Possession" crimes and their penalties are defined in Conn. Gen. Stat. § 21a-279. Sale or Distribution crimes and their penalties are defined in Conn. Gen. Stat. § 21a-278 (non-drug dependent) and § 21a-277 (drug dependent) respectively.

For certain categories of highly addictive drugs (narcotics, amphetamines, and hallucinogens), Connecticut has chosen to impose lighter prison sentences in lieu of treatment and rehabilitation for a defendant deemed to be "drug dependent" at the time of their sale or attempted sale of a controlled substance. The legislature has separated the crime of "sale or distribution of a controlled substance" into two sections (§§21a-277 & 21a-278). Conn. Gen. Stat. § 21a-277 covers the "penalty for illegal manufacture, distribution, sale, prescription, dispensing," while Conn. Gen. Stat. § 21a-278 covers the "penalty for illegal manufacture, distribution, sale, prescription or administration by a non-drug-dependent person." 21a-278 includes those highly addictive drugs and includes enhanced penalties for possessing significant amounts of those drugs that the legislature has deemed inappropriate for someone who is deemed a drug dependent person. In other words, more than is necessary for your own, personal use.

In addition to these basic crimes, Connecticut seeks to protect the interests of children with the aggravating offenses contained in Conn. Gen. Stat. § 21a-278a. These offenses, selling to a person under 18 years of age, selling within 1,500 feet of a school zone, and employing a person under 18 to sell, all carry mandatory minimum sentences to be added onto any penalties for the underlying offense. In some cities, there is hardly a single square block radius that is not within 1,500 feet of some type of school or other educational institution, making sale of narcotics anywhere in that city an enhanced crime. This offense carries a mandatory minimum period of incarceration of three years.

Common drug crimes in Connecticut are as follows:

Controlled Substances

Such a simple name – but so many variations that could cause criminal problems in Connecticut. For the most part, controlled substances are either illegal drugs, like cocaine, heroin, methamphetamine, and crack, or legal drugs that must be prescribed by a doctor. In either situation, there are rules about who can have them, how much they can have, and when they can get them, hence the term "controlled substances."

While controlled substances is a simple term that doesn't really explain what they are, there are different classifications for controlled substances set forth by the federal government, and used by the state. They set forth schedules of where drugs should be classified into five different listings.

Schedule I Substances

The drugs in this schedule are those that have no accepted medical use in the United States and have a high abuse potential. Some examples are heroin, marijuana, LSD, peyote, mescaline, psilocybin, and others. Many of these drugs are commonly called hallucinogens. While marijuana is classified as a Schedule I drug, it has been accepted as having a medical use in Connecticut and in other states, but the federal government has not changed its classification yet.

In Connecticut, if you are a resident who has been diagnosed with a medical disorder for which you may be prescribed marijuana as a treatment, you may apply for a medical marijuana card. A medical marijuana card will enable you to possess marijuana up to the amount that is granted on your card in its original dispensary container without being charged criminally in state court.

Schedule II Substances

The drugs in this schedule have a high abuse potential with psychic or physical dependence liability. Schedule II controlled substances consist of certain narcotic, stimulant, and depressant drugs. Some examples of Schedule II controlled narcotic substances are: opium, morphine, codeine, Dilaudid, methadone, cocaine, and oxycodone. Also in Schedule II are amphetamine and methamphetamine. Since crack is a derivation of cocaine, it falls into this category.

Schedule III, IV and V drugs are very rare in Connecticut so we won't go into them, but if you want more information, you can contact us.

Next, let's talk about drug possession. Connecticut Statutes define "possess" as having physical possession or otherwise to exercise dominion or control over tangible property. Conn. Gen. Stat. § 53a-3(2). The crime of "illegal possession of a controlled substance" means certain things. It refers to an intentional control of the controlled substance accompanied by knowledge of its character.

The crime of illegal possession of a controlled substance has three separate "elements." The state must prove these elements beyond a reasonable doubt.

Illegal Possession of a Controlled Substance – Elements:

- Element One: The defendant knew the character of the substance;
- Element Two: The defendant knew of its presence;
- Element Three: The defendant exercised dominion and control over it.

The first two elements concern the mental intent of the defendant to intentionally possess a controlled substance. The third element requires that the defendant express "dominion and control" over the substance: actual "possession." However, this does not mean that someone has to actually possess the drug in the ordinary sense of the word to be guilty of violating § 21a-279.

The legal concept of "exercising dominion and control" over a controlled substance does not require actually having the substance on one's person. Instead, it refers to the act of having a position of control coupled with the requisite mental state. In addition, depending on facts of a particular case, a jury may infer that a defendant knew of a drug's character and presence from the fact that the defendant possessed the substance.

Constructive Possession

Possession of a controlled substance may be actual, or it may be constructive. Although both actual and constructive possession require the elements of knowledge and control described in the previous section, the concept of constructive possession involves the situation in which the defendant, although not in actual possession of the substance, (e.g., it is not on their person or so close to them as to be functionally on their person) knowingly has the power and the intention of exercising dominion and control over the substance.

A major factor in determining whether an individual has constructive possession of contraband is whether or not they are in exclusive possession of the premises on which that contraband is found. No minimum amount of illegal substance must exist to constitute illegal possession; even a trace amount or residue will suffice.

Now let's focus on marijuana, because it is unique. It is not yet legal in the state of Connecticut to buy and use marijuana for recreational purposes. It is legal to be prescribed marijuana as a therapeutic drug for specific medical diagnoses, and you will be permitted to purchase a controlled amount at a dispensary.

Marijuana has been decriminalized in Connecticut, specifically for adults and in small amounts. Possession of under one-half ounce of marijuana is punishable by a fine. This is comparable to most driving violations because similarly, you receive a speeding ticket and pay a fine if you are caught speeding, not sent to jail. But if you are under 21, you will face a driver's license suspension as a consequence of the offense.

Many times, the police do not keep the suspected marijuana and, therefore it cannot be confirmed. In that case, you may be able to win with that argument alone.

"Sale" is a pretty simple concept at first blush, but it doesn't always come down to the exchange of money for drugs. The reality is that even giving someone a controlled substance is enough for sale. You don't have to be paid for the drugs for a sale to take place. Also, merely by the amount of drug present, the police can determine that a sale or intent to sell has taken place. This is why it is so important to have a drug defense lawyer on your side when facing drug charges in Connecticut.

Chapter 9:

Pleas, Trials and Sentencing

When facing a criminal charge, it is common to only think about how it will end and it can be overwhelming to think about the steps in between. For many, the use of a diversionary program, the focus of our next chapter, may get your case settled. For others, a trial may be the best course of action, but for some a plea may be in order.

Pleas of guilty can take three forms. The first type of guilty plea is a straight guilty plea. These pleas are exactly what they say they are. You admit to the charges as agreed upon with the state and confess guilt for them. These pleas are done in open court and you will forever have a criminal record for the convictions. In fact, in all situations you will have a conviction record and that record could have collateral consequences on firearms rights, immigration status, applications for employment and school, among other things.

The second type of plea is an Alford plea. This is based on the case of North Carolina vs. Alford. The holding of this case established that the defendant can plead guilty without admitting guilt. The defendant can disagree with some or even all of the facts that the state is alleging, but wants to take the offer that is on the table, rather than risking a worse punishment after trial, where the state could convince the judge or jury that the defendant is guilty. This is something clients will choose to do if they do not wish to agree with everything that the state may claim they did.

The final type of plea is a no contest. The official term for this is nolo contendere, which is Latin for "no contest." This means that while you have heard the state's allegations, you are choosing not to fight them at all. This means you do not say the word guilty, but the judge will find you guilty.

The nolo contendere plea is a written plea that must follow a specific format. It is often used in cases where there is a potential civil lawsuit from the damages of the act, because while a guilty plea can be used against you in a civil lawsuit, a nolo plea cannot, so it makes the job of the civil lawyer trying to sue you a little harder.

Now, this nolo plea should not be confused with another Latin phrase which is used a lot, which is "nolle prosequi," colloquially known as a "nolle" in Connecticut, or "nol pros" in some other states. In a nolle, the state is choosing not to prosecute the case against you, and in 13 months, the court will automatically order it dismissed. A nolle may be reopened any time within that 13 month period to resume prosecution. When the state chooses to nolle a case, the defense does have the ability to object to a nolle to insist on a trial or move for a dismissal, but sometimes that is not wise if it is a negotiated nolle, so a criminal defense lawyer is your best advisor in this situation.

Whenever a person resolves a case with a plea there will be something called a "canvas." This is a question and answer session with a judge in the courtroom, on the record, when the judge will ask the defendant a series of questions to make sure they are entering the plea knowing all of the rights they are giving up in exchange for the plea and are making the decision with the effective advice of counsel. The canvas has certain questions that have to be asked and answered, so a lawyer will prepare you for this. In felony cases, a canvas must be done, but in misdemeanor cases it can be waived. For the most part, judges want to canvas even on misdemeanor cases.

There are a few different things that can occur once the case has resolved. The most serious consequence is straight jail time. Straight jail time sounds exactly like what it is. You are sentenced to a period of jail time and you have to serve it. It is "flat" time and when you are done with your jail time, you are out and free again with no post-release supervision. This is a rare sentence and usually only done in the most serious of cases when the sentence is for the rest of the person's life or for habitual offenders, who know the system well and know that they are unlikely to be successful on probation.

The next option is a split sentence. This is a situation where you are sentenced to a period of jail time and a period of probation. Now, a split sentence has to have a period of jail time "suspended" which means it hangs over your head while you are on probation. If you violate your probation, you can be rearrested and are then exposed to the suspended jail time.

Let's explain it in context. If a person gets a split sentence of 5/2/3, it means that the person has five years in jail as a sentence, but the execution of that sentence is suspended after they serve only two of those years in jail. After that time, they are released and then serve on probation for three years. If they violate the probation at any time in the three year period, they could be made to serve the additional two years that were suspended.

Now, some sentences are split in that the jail sentence for three years (or any amount of time) is totally suspended with probation. This means that there will be no jail time upfront, and the time hanging over your head exists to give you incentive to successfully complete probation.

For the most part, probations for misdemeanors cannot exceed two years, and for felonies cannot exceed five years, but they can be longer for certain offenses, such as sex offenses, probation for which is often ten years to match the length of time the defendant is made to register as a sex offender.

Finally, there are dispositions that include only a fine, which are rare, and even more rare is the guilty plea with no fine, sentence, or probation. Even though this result is rare, it does happen.

The concepts of sentencing are very complicated, and anyone contemplating jail time should really speak with an attorney about the collateral consequences and all of the parts of the plea canvas. Approximately 95% of all state criminal cases resolve prior to a trial, and there's a reason for that - the risk of going to trial is often severe. If you lose at trial, you are then exposed to the maximum periods of incarceration for each offense, which can run consecutively (or one after the other). To avoid that risk, defendants negotiate with the prosecutor to enter guilty pleas.

If you have a loved one who has a case, we are happy to speak about all the different variations and what could happen. But remember, 100% of the people who plead guilty are found guilty, and sometimes the only way to win a case is to be prepared to go the distance for a trial. It may not be the cheapest option, but long term it may be much cheaper than living with a conviction.

Chapter 10:

Diversionary Programs

For the most part, a diversionary program allows you to avoid entering a guilty plea, and asks the court to place you on a period of supervision. This usually happens by a division of Court Support Services, and allows you to earn a dismissal of the charges. You may earn that dismissal by doing counseling, doing community service, or sometimes merely just staying out of trouble.

One of the biggest challenges for many of these programs is that you only get one chance to use them in your lifetime, so you don't want to use them unless you absolutely must, because many people like to keep them available for the future. Because the judge must find that you are not likely to offend again for many diversionary programs, it becomes a tough argument to tell a prosecutor that you want to "save" your program for the "next time" you might need it, but there is often a situation where you can have your case resolved another way that protects you from wasting a program. Remember, a prosecutor does not have to tell you that they cannot prove the case against you or that the police did something wrong and can offer you a diversionary program to resolve your case. This is sometimes done to protect bad cops and bad cases, and unless you know what to look for, you might hurt yourself long term by accepting a diversionary program when you shouldn't.

Long story short, you should always speak to a defense lawyer before opting into one of these programs.

In the rest of this chapter, we will outline the common diversionary programs available in Connecticut. They include the Accelerated Pretrial Rehabilitation Program (AR), Pretrial Supervised Diversionary Program For Persons With Psychiatric Disabilities (Psych AR/SDP), Pretrial Drug Education and Community Service Program (DEP), Connecticut Alcohol and Drug Abuse Counseling Program (CADAC), Pretrial Alcohol Education Program (AEP), Pretrial Family Violence Education Program (Family Violence), Youthful Offender Program (YO), Pretrial School Violence Education Program (School Violence), and the Community Service Labor Program (CSLP).

ACCELERATED PRETRIAL REHABILITATION (AR) CONN. GEN. STAT. §54-56E

What is It?

The Accelerated Pretrial Rehabilitation Program (AR) is for defendants and veterans who are charged with certain crimes or motor vehicle violations that may lead to incarceration. The purpose of AR is to give first time offenders a second chance and an opportunity to avoid criminal conviction. Certain requirements are outlined below to determine if you are eligible to participate in AR. If the court finds you to be eligible and grants the application, it will then determine the proper program and conditions necessary. This could include community services, restitution payments, psychiatric or psychological counseling, alcohol and/or drug treatment, an animal cruelty prevention and education program, or a hate crimes diversion program. The Court Support Services Division (CSSD) will supervise your progress. If you follow all conditions required by the court and finish the AR program successfully, charges against you will be dismissed.

Step 1 - Who is Eligible?

The following people are eligible for the AR program:

- Any person charged with a crime or motor vehicle violations that is not of a serious nature but could be sentenced to imprisonment (excluding family violence offenses and most sex offenses);
- A and B felonies are excluded from eligibility, except for certain Class B felonies. Certain Class B felonies included are limited to:
    - § 53a-122(a)(1), (2) or (3) - Larceny 1st, which does not involve use, attempted use or threatened use of physical force against another; or
    - § 53a-122(a)(4) - Larceny 1st, which does not involve the use, attempted use, or

threatened use of physical force against another person and does not involve a violation by a person who is a public official, as defined in section 1-110, or a state or municipal employee as defined in section 1-110.

- Class C felonies, but only where the court finds good cause;
- Any person the court believes will most likely not offend in the future;
- Any person that has no previous record of a conviction of a crime or a violation of:
    - § 14-196 - Fraud related to a certificate of title or ownership instrument;
    - § 14-215(c) - Operation of a motor vehicle with a suspended license;
    - § 14-222a - Negligent homicide with a motor vehicle;
    - § 14-224(a) and § 114-224(b)(1) - Evading responsibility of an accident involving serious physical injury/death;
    - § 14-227a - Operating under the influence of alcohol or drugs.

Step 2 - Application Process

You may apply for AR by filing a standard court form in court. Afterwards, the judge will ask you a number of questions - namely if you have used the program before and if you waive their rights to a speedy trial. You must agree to a tolling of the statute of limitations. This allows the state more time to prosecute if the program is not successfully completed.

If you want to take advantage of AR, you will be required to pay a $35 application fee. The court file is then sealed. This means that the general public will not be able to see what you are charged with.

If there are any victims of the crime for which you are charged, you are required to send a notice to the victim to inform them of the AR application. This is done by certified mail so it can be proven that the victim was given notice. The victim will have a chance to offer their opinion and be heard in court.

Once these steps are completed, the Court Support Services (CSSD) will conduct an investigation to determine your eligibility.

Step 3 - Admittance to the Program

If admitted into the program, you must pay a program fee of $100. The length of the program will vary based on the facts and circumstances of each case (one day to two years). You must appear in court to be released into the custody of the Court Support Services Division (CSSD), and the period of probation or supervision by the CSSD may not exceed two years. If you fail to follow the conditions set by the court, the program will be terminated unsuccessfully and the case will be brought back on the docket for prosecution, ending either in a plea or a trial.

Step 4 - Successful Completion of the AR Program

You may apply for dismissal of the charges, which shall be granted by the court after verification of program completion. If you do not apply for dismissal, the court may make its own motion and dismiss charges upon receipt of program completion. Upon approval and dismissal, all records of the charges and arrest shall be erased pursuant to the Connecticut Erasure Statute Conn. Gen. Stat. § 54-142a.

Special Conditions

Special conditions for AR include:

- If the defendant is older than 16 but younger than 18, the defendant may be referred to the Youth Services Bureau;
- Certain offenses may lead the court to require the defendant to participate in a Hate Crimes Diversion Program; those are:
    - § 46a-58 - Deprivation of Rights; Desecration of Property; Placing of Burning Cross or Noose;
    - § 53-37a - Deprivation of a person's civil rights while wearing hood;
    - § 53a-181j - Intimidation Based on Bigotry or Bias 1st;

  - § 53a-181k - Intimidation Based on Bigotry or Bias 2nd;
  - § 53a-181l - Intimidation Based on Bigotry or Bias 3rd.
- The Hate Crimes Diversion Program requirement has a larger fee of $425;
  - The defendant may attend a similar program in another state if the fee is paid in Connecticut and the court approves. An out-of-state program must include an educational program and supervised community service.

PRETRIAL SUPERVISED DIVERSIONARY PROGRAM FOR PERSONS WITH PSYCHIATRIC DISABILITIES (PSYCH AR/SDP) CONN. GEN. STAT. § 54-56L

What is It?

The Pretrial Supervised Diversionary Program for Persons with Psychiatric Disabilities, also informally called Psych AR, is for defendants who have psychiatric disabilities or who are veterans, and have been charged with crimes or motor vehicle violations that may result in incarceration. "Psychiatric disabilities" is defined as a mental or emotional condition, other than solely substance abuse, that has substantial adverse effects on the ability to function and requires care and treatment. Veterans who are eligible must be veterans with a mental health condition who is amenable to treatment, if they were not dishonorably discharged or released from the military. For the purpose of this book, we will abbreviate the acronym not using the offensive term Psych AR but use the abbreviation envisioned by the statute - SDP.

The purpose of the program is to provide a tailored treatment plan for those who need mental health treatment as well as an opportunity to avoid criminal conviction. Certain requirements are outlined below to determine if you are eligible to participate in SDP. If the court finds you to be eligible and grants the application, the Court Support Services Division (CSSD) will determine the proper treatment and services to provide to you. The CSSD will supervise your treatment and progress. If you follow all conditions required by the court and complete the SDP program successfully, charges against you will be dismissed.

Step 1 - Who is Eligible?

Those eligible for this program include:

- Any person with a psychiatric disability or who is a veteran, charged with a crime or motor vehicle violation that is not of a serious nature but could be sentenced to imprisonment;
- Any person eligible to participate in Accelerated Rehabilitation (AR) or the Pretrial Family Violence Education Program, if the court finds participation in this supervised diversionary program is more appropriate;

- Any person who has not twice previously participated in a supervised diversionary program.

Step 2 - Application Process

To apply for the SDP program, you must submit your application with the court. Then you state, under oath and in open court, that you have not participated in the program more than once. Just as with AR, you must agree to a tolling of the statute of limitations. This allows the state more time to prosecute if the program is not successfully completed. In addition, you must waive your right to a speedy trial. The court will then seal the court file.

If there are any victims of the crime that you are charged with, court personnel shall have a notice sent to any victim(s). All victims will have an opportunity to share their opinion and be heard by the court.

Then, you will be referred to the Court Support Services Division (CSSD) to confirm eligibility and assess your mental health condition. A copy of the police record will be provided to CSSD by the prosecutor. You will be referred to an evaluation with the Department of Mental Health and Addiction Services (DHMAS) to determine whether you suffer from a mental health disorder for which treatment is recommended, and recommend treatment which may include inpatient or outpatient treatment, and may include medication. If CSSD is able to determine that appropriate services are available, then a treatment plan will be tailored to you and presented to the court.

Step 3 - Admittance to the SDP Program

If the court grants your application into the program, you will then be referred to CSSD for monitoring the compliance with recommended treatment. The CSSD may coordinate with the Department of Mental Health and Addiction Services, (DMHAS), the Department of Veteran's Affairs, or the United States Department of Veteran Affairs to place you in a program with appropriate supervision, treatment, and services. CSSD will notify the victim(s) of any conditions that directly affects the victim as well as scheduled court appearances.

Depending on the facts and circumstances of the case, the judge may order you in the program for a period of up to three years. You must agree to any conditions established by the CSSD concerning participation in the program, including program meetings and/or sessions. If you are ineligible or fail to successfully complete the program, the court will terminate the program as unsuccessful, unseal the file, enter a plea of not guilty, and the case will be referred for further prosecution.

Step 4 - Successful Completion of the SDP Program

You may apply for dismissal of the charges, which shall be granted by the court after verification of program completion. If you do not apply for dismissal, the court may make its own motion and dismiss charges upon receipt of program completion. Upon approval and dismissal, all records of the charges shall be erased.

The CSSD will retain your information for five years, including your name, date of birth, social security number, violation(s) charged, dates of program participation, and any weapons/dangerous instruments involved in charged violations. All information will be available to state and local police officers. All police reports and records of supervision will be retained by the CSSD and available to both prosecution and defense counsel if the court is considering granting the application for a participant a second time.

PRETRIAL DRUG EDUCATION AND COMMUNITY SERVICE PROGRAM (DEP) CONN. GEN. STAT. §54-56l

What is It?

The purpose of the Pretrial Drug Education and Community Service Program ("DEP") is to provide defendants with beneficial options and resources. The educational part of the program is designed to inform people of the lasting effects drugs have on health, personal relationships, and behavior. There is also a community service component to the program. The DEP allows individuals to learn and grow as well as an opportunity to dismiss the charges against them. The court's requirements for participation in the program are outlined below. If the court finds you to be eligible and grants the application, you will be evaluated to determine proper treatment and services. This can range from either 10 or 15 drug education classes, to substance abuse treatment in the case of more severe drug addictions. Your treatment and progress will be supervised and if all requirements are completed, charges against you will be dismissed.

Step 1 - Who is Eligible?

Those eligible for DEP include:

- Any persons charged with:
    - § 21a-267 - Use, possession/deliverance of drug paraphernalia;
    - § 21a-279 - Possession of a controlled substance; or
    - § 21a-279a - Possession of less than ½ an ounce of a cannabis type substance.
- Any person who has not participated in the following programs twice:
    - The Drug Education Program (DEP) as it existed before October 1st, 2013;
    - The Pretrial Community Service Labor Program (CSLP) under §53a-39c;
    - The DEP.

Although you are not eligible for the program if you are charged with Possession with Intent to Sell (PWITS) under § 21a-277, we may be able to negotiate with the prosecutor to file amended charges to allow for entrance into the program. You should contact a criminal defense attorney to determine if this is possible in your case.

Step 2 - Application Process

Those who wish to participate in this program must submit an application to the court, pay a $100 application fee, and pay a $150 evaluation fee. The court will then seal the file from the public. The state prosecution will have an opportunity to offer an opinion to the court, and if the court denies the application, the file will be unsealed, a plea of not guilty will be entered, and the prosecution will proceed, although the case is almost never placed directly on the trial list.

Step 3 - Admittance to the Program

Upon admittance to the DEP, you must pay a $600 program fee. If the court orders substance abuse treatment, you must pay a $100 program fee. In addition, any person may request that part or all of the fee be waived if an affidavit of indigence/inability is filed and confirmed with the court, but keep in mind that once paid, fees are nonrefundable.

In addition, you must agree to a tolling of the statute of limitations and waiving of right to a speedy trial. This allows the state more time to prosecute if the program is not successfully completed. The length of the program will vary based on the specific facts and requirements of each case, but will not exceed one year.

You must agree to accept placement in a treatment program and complete participation in the program. You will be referred to the Court Support Services Division (CSSD) to confirm eligibility. You will also be referred to the Department of Mental Health and Addiction Services (DMHAS) for an evaluation and determination of appropriate drug education and treatment for a first or second time application. Alternatively, you may be referred to a state licensed substance abuse treatment program for evaluation and determination of appropriate drug education and treatment for a third time application. If you are a veteran, the Department of Veterans' Affairs or United States Department of Veterans' Affairs will be notified for evaluation. "Veterans" are considered those who were discharged or released under conditions other than dishonorable from active service in the armed forces.

Once eligibility is confirmed and evaluations are received, you will be placed in the program and referred by the CSSD to the proper program placement. Only licensed facilities in full compliance with state standards are allowed to provide treatment related to this program.

You must also participate in community service. First time participants are required to complete five days of community service, second time participants must complete 15 days, and third time participants must complete 30 days.

Participation in the DEP program shall not exceed one year. If you are ineligible or fail to successfully complete the program, the court will unseal the file, enter a plea of not guilty, and prosecution on the case will proceed.

Step 4 - Successful Completion of the DEP Program

Upon completion of the program, you may apply for dismissal of the charges, which shall be granted by the court after verification of program completion. If you do not apply for dismissal, the court may make its own motion and dismiss charges upon receipt of program completion. Upon approval and dismissal, all records of the charges shall be dismissed. The court may extend the placement period for a reasonable time at the participant's request if good cause is shown. Finally, the CSSD will retain your program participation records for 10 years.

CONNECTICUT ALCOHOL AND DRUG ABUSE COUNSELING PROGRAM (CADAC) CONN. GEN. STAT. §§ 17A-691 - 17A-701

What is It?

The purpose of the Connecticut Alcohol and Drug Abuse Counseling Program (CADAC) is to help individuals struggling with an alcohol or drug dependency. The treatment program will be tailored to the individual to help them find independence from their alcohol and/or drug dependency. Completion of the program may lead to a recommendation by the Court Support System Division (CSSD) to dismiss charges against the defendant. For convicted individuals who are able to participate and complete CADAC, an opportunity to modify their sentence, terms of probation, or even terminate probation is possible.

Step 1 - Who is Eligible?

People eligible for CADAC include:

- Any person charged with a crime, that is drug or alcohol dependent, and eligible for treatment;
- The program is not available to defendants charged with:
    - A Class A, B, or C felony;
    - § 14-2227a - Operating under the influence of alcohol or drugs; or
    - § 53a-60d - Assault 2nd with a motor vehicle.
- The program is not available to defendants who have been treated under this program twice before;
- The court may choose to waive the defendant's ineligibility if it chooses, in limited circumstances.

Step 2 - Application Process

The court, prosecutor, or defense counsel can file a motion for an examination to determine if a person charged with a crime has a drug or alcohol dependency. The court will then seal the file from the public. In addition, the commissioner of the Department of Mental Health and Addictive Services (DMHAS) will appoint one or more clinical examiners to conduct an examination. The examiner(s) will determine if you are likely to benefit from treatment and deliver a report and recommendation to the court.

If there are any victims of the crime for which you are charged, you are required to send a notice to the victim(s) to inform them of the motion to suspend prosecution. Upon receiving notice, the victim will have a chance to offer their opinion and be heard in court.

In order to apply for the CADAC program, you must pay a $25 fee. If the motion is denied, the State may proceed with prosecution against you.

Step 3 - Admittance to the CADAC Program

In the event that a person is admitted to the CADAC program, they are responsible for the cost of treatment. You must also agree to a tolling of the statute of limitations and waive your right to a speedy trial. Time will vary based on program requirements, but will not exceed two years.

You will be placed into the custody of CSSD, where CSSD will monitor any violations, violence, refusals to participate, request for removal, or inability to participate. These issues are reported to the court clerk.

Treatment will begin when the clinical examiner reports available space in the program. If the court terminates the suspension period or the motion is dismissed, the state may commence prosecution.

Step 4 - Successful Completion of the CADAC Program

Once the program is successfully completed, you will be discharged from treatment. CSSD will notify the court of completed treatment and submit a report including your status and a recommendation. Completion of the program, compliance to CSSD required conditions, and one-year abstinence from drugs and alcohol are required for a dismissal recommendation.

The court may dismiss charges if you have completed the treatment program, are responding well to treatment, and have complied with all conditions required during suspension of prosecution.

PRETRIAL ALCOHOL EDUCATION PROGRAM (AEP) CONN. GEN. STAT. § 54-56G

What is It?

The Pretrial Alcohol Education Program (AEP) is designed for defendants facing DUI charges. The program allows the defendant to participate in classes and treatment as recommended after an evaluation. Upon successful completion of the program, the court will dismiss the charges against the defendant, with only a notation of program participation on their driving record.

Step 1 - Who is Eligible?

Those eligible for the AEP are any defendant charged with:

- § 14-227a - Operating a motor vehicle under the influence of alcohol or drugs;
- § 14-227g - Operating a motor vehicle by a person under the age of 21 with BAC above 1/200%;
- § 15-113 - Operating a vessel while under the influence of alcohol or drugs;
- § 15-140n - Reckless operation of a vessel 2nd while under the influence of alcohol or drugs.
- You do NOT hold a CDL license in this state or any other state.

Step 2 - Application Process

You must submit an application with the court if you would like to apply for AEP. You must pay a $100 application fee and a $100 evaluation fee. The court will then seal the file from the public.

If there are any victims of the crime that you are charged with, court personnel shall have notice sent to any victim(s). All victims will have an opportunity to share their opinion about you using this diversionary program and be heard by the court. If the court denies the application, you are ineligible, or fail to successfully complete the program, the court will unseal the file, enter a plea of not guilty, and refer the case for continued prosecution.

Step 3 - Admittance to the AEP

If admitted to the AEP, you must pay a program fee of $350 for a ten-session program or a fee of $500 for a fifteen-session program. If substance abuse treatment is ordered by the court, you are responsible for the cost of the program. However, part or all of the fees may be waived if an indigence/inability affidavit is submitted and confirmed by the court.

You will be referred to the Court Support Services Division (CSSD) for eligibility and will then be referred to the Department of Mental Health and Addiction Services (DMHAS) for an evaluation. DMHAS will determine appropriate placement into an alcohol intervention program or a state licensed substance abuse treatment program, and placement will be for one year.

You must agree to the following in order to participate in the AEP:

- A tolling of the statute of limitations;
- Waive the right to a speedy trial;
- Accept DMHAS placement;
- Complete the program ordered by the court.

You must begin the program within 90 days of application approval by the court. CSSD will notify the court if you fail to complete the program. If this is the case, the court will then unseal the file, enter a plea of not guilty, and place the case on the trial list.

You may request reinstatement if still eligible, but should keep in mind that fees are associated with reinstatement and you cannot be reinstated more than twice.

Step 4 - Successful Completion of the AEP

Upon successful completion of the AEP, you may apply for dismissal of the charges, which shall be granted by the court after verification of program completion. If you do not apply for dismissal, the court may make its own motion and dismiss charges upon receipt of completion. The CSSD will retain a record of your participation in the program for two years. This record will be sent to the Department of Motor Vehicles where it will also be retained for 10 years. Finally, records of certain charges will be sent to the Department of Environmental Protection, where they will be retained for 10 years.

PRETRIAL FAMILY VIOLENCE EDUCATION PROGRAM (FAMILY VIOLENCE OR FVEP) CONN. GEN. STAT. §§ 46B-38A - 46B-38F

What is It?

This program is designed for defendants facing domestic violence charges. The goal is to provide first time offenders with resources to understand their violent behavior and actions that led to the charges, and determine healthy and effective techniques of communication. Upon completion of the program, within six months to one year, charges against the defendant will be dismissed.

Step 1 - Who is Eligible?

The following people are eligible for the Family Violence Program:

- Defendants involved in an incident resulting in:
    - Bodily harm/injury;
    - Assault;
    - Stalking;
    - Pattern of threats/threatened violence.
- Defendants who have not previously:
    - Been convicted of a family violence offense on/after October 1st, 1986;
    - Used the Family Violence Program in the past;
    - Used the Accelerated Rehabilitation Program for family violence offense on/after October 1st, 1986.
- Defendants who have not been charged with:
    - Unclassified felony with a penalty of 10 years imprisonment;
    - Class D or unclassified felony carrying less than five year exposure (unless good cause can be shown);
    - Inflicting serious physical injury (as defined in section 53a-3).

Step 2 - Application Process

If you would like to take advantage of the Family Violence Program, you must apply through the court. You must answer the judge's questions, under oath and on record.

If there are any victims of the crime for which you are charged, you are required to send a notice to the victim to inform them of the program application. The victim(s) will have a chance to offer their opinion and be heard in court.

Step 3 - Admittance to the Family Violence Program

If admitted to this program, you must agree to:

- Tolling of statute of limitations;
- Waive your right to a speedy trial;
- Pay a $300 Program Fee.

A court representative will monitor your progress in the program, and you must participate in nine, 90 minute educational sessions.

Step 4 - Successful Completion of the Family Violence Program

Once the program is completed, you may apply for dismissal of the charges, which shall be granted by the court after verification of program completion. If you do not apply for dismissal, the court may make its own motion and dismiss charges upon receipt of completion of the program. The protective order will remain in effect during the length of the program and will be dismissed at the same time as the program upon successful completion.

YOUTHFUL OFFENDER (YO) CONN. GEN. STAT. §§ 54-76B - 54-76O

What is It?

Defendants who are older than sixteen but younger than eighteen and facing criminal charges may qualify as "Youthful Offenders" (YO). This qualification allows special procedures to be implemented during court proceedings. Greater confidentiality is placed on the records related to the case, and once the defendant reaches the age of 21 the records are erased, as long as the defendant does not commit a subsequent felony prior to turning 21.

Step 1 - Who is Eligible?

The following people are eligible for YO status:

- Defendant older than 16, but younger than 18;
- Defendants who have NOT been charged with:
  - Class A felony;
  - § 14-222a - Negligent Homicide with a Motor Vehicle;
  - § 14-224(a) or (b)(1) - Evading where serious physical injury or death results;
  - § 14-227a - Operating of motor vehicle under the influence of alcohol or drugs;
  - § 14-227g - Operating of motor vehicle by a person under the age of 21 with BAC above 1/200%;

- § 53-21(a)(2) - Intimate contact of or with a child under the age of 16;
- § 53a- 70 - Sexual Assault 1st;
- § 53a-70a - Aggravated Sexual Assault 1st;
- § 53a-71 - Sexual Assault 2nd;
- § 53a-72a - Sexual Assault 3rd;
- § 53a-72b - Sexual Assault 3rd with a Firearm;
- Except: Acts of consensual sexual intercourse or contact with the defendant and a person older than 13 years old, but younger than 16 years old;
- The defendant has not been previously convicted of a felony on a regular criminal docket;
- Previously adjudged a serious juvenile offender;
- A serious juvenile repeat offender.

Step 2 - Application Process

If not charged with any of the offenses listed above, the court presumes that you qualify for YO status. In this case, your file will be sealed from the public. If no motion is made by the state, you will be deemed eligible. At this point, you must enter a guilty plea. All proceedings are private within the court, but if there is a victim involved in the case, they must be allowed access to the proceedings.

The court will then determine proper action, which may include:

- A fine (not more than $1,000);
- To commit you;
- Imposing a sentence of conditional/unconditional discharge;
- Imposing community service;
- Imposing a sentence to a term of imprisonment;
- Imposing probation;
- Ordering treatment/counseling;
- Referring you to the Youth Services Bureau.

Step 3 - Ramifications for Adjudication Youthful Offenders

You are not impaired from holding any public office, public employment, or right to receive any license. In addition, all records and information will be confidential and sealed and all proceedings are conducted in a courtroom closed to the public, with only the parties and your guardian present. However, these records may be:

- Provided to the State Police Bureau of Identification;
- Provided to the Division of State Police within the Department of Public Safety;
- Disclosed to individuals and agencies directly providing services to youth;
- Available to parents/guardians of youth;
- Available to representing counsel;

- Available to victim to the extent available in a regular criminal docket;
- Any records of motor vehicle violations will be disclosed to the Department of Motor Vehicles.

All records and police reports will be deleted automatically when you turn 21 years old, as long as you do not commit a subsequent felony before turning 21. Your information will be removed from all agencies, again, assuming that you do not commit another felony before age 21. You will have no record of arrest for the offense.

PRETRIAL SCHOOL VIOLENCE EDUCATION PROGRAM (SCHOOL VIOLENCE) CONN. GEN. STAT. § 54-56J

What is It?

Defendants charged with an offense involving the use or threatened use of physical violence in or on school property are eligible to participate in the Pretrial School Violence Education Program, also known as the School Violence Program. The program allows defendants to attend group counseling in anger management and nonviolent conflict resolution. The Court Support Services Division (CSSD) will track the defendant's progress and participation. After successful completion of the program, the court will dismiss the charges.

Step 1 - Who is Eligible?

Defendants charged with an offense involving use or threatened use of physical violence in or on public/private school property or school sponsored activity are eligible for the program. The student must attend a public or private secondary school.

Step 2 - Application Process

You must apply for this program with the court. You and your parents/guardians state under oath in open court that you are not in possession of any firearms, dangerous weapons, controlled substances, or other property prohibited. Then the State will have the opportunity to be heard before a decision is reached. If you are deemed ineligible, the file will be unsealed, a plea of not guilty will be entered, and the case will be referred for further prosecution.

Step 3 - Admittance to the Program

On the other hand, if you are deemed eligible and admitted to the program, your parents/guardians must pay the program cost. Then you are referred to the CSSD to confirm eligibility. Once confirmed, an evaluation is conducted and proper placement will be determined.

You must agree to:

- A tolling of the statute of limitations;
- Waive your right to a speedy trial;
- Participate and attend the program for one year;

- Successfully complete the program.

The program will consist of at least eight group counseling sessions in anger management and nonviolent conflict resolution. In addition, the CSSD will monitor your progress and participation and will notify the court of failure to complete the program. If the program is not successfully completed, the court will unseal the file, enter a plea of not guilty, and place the case on the trial list.

Step 4 - Successful Completion of the Program

You may apply for a dismissal of charges after successfully completing the program and after one year has elapsed since you began the program. Once the court has verified completion, the court will dismiss the charges. If you do not apply for dismissal, but have completed the program and one year has elapsed, the court may file its own motion and dismiss the charges once it has verified completion.

COMMUNITY SERVICE LABOR PROGRAM (CSLP) CONN. GEN. STAT. § 53A-39C

What is It?

The Community Service Labor Program (CSLP) was created for individuals convicted of drug possession offenses. Defendants may apply to participate in the program for a chance to provide community service rather than serve a term of imprisonment. If the court grants the defendant's application, a guilty plea is entered without a trial and the imprisonment term is suspended upon the condition of successful completion of the program.

Step 1 - Who is Eligible?

The following people are eligible for the CSLP:

- Defendants who have never previously been convicted of:
  - § 21a-277 - Illegal manufacture, distribution, sale, prescription or dispensing controlled substances; or
  - § 21a-278 - Illegal manufacture, distribution, sale, prescription or dispensing controlled substances by a non-drug dependent person.
- Defendants who have been convicted of a drug possession offense as a first offense.
- Defendants that have not previously participated in CSLP.

Step 2 - Application Process

You may submit an application through the court if you want to participate in the CSLP.

Step 3 - Admittance to the Program

If the court grants the application, you must plead guilty without a trial and pay a $205 participation fee. If admitted to the program, the term of imprisonment will be suspended with the condition of successful completion of the program. Participation in the CSLP program will be for 30 days.

Step 4 - Successful Completion

Upon successful completion of the program, your term of imprisonment is waived.

Chapter 11:

Violation of Probation

Violations of probation are serious cases. They are serious because the burden for proving them is much lower than a normal criminal case. In the first chapter of this book, we talked about the levels of proof in criminal cases. You may recall that we talked about how reasonable articulable suspicion is the first step on the staircase to reaching proof beyond all reasonable doubt. We used the staircase analogy because it is easy to understand that the prosecution must "climb the staircase" to reach their burden. The second step on the staircase is probable cause. The next step in a criminal case is beyond a reasonable doubt; but in a violation of probation case there is actually a step in between probable cause and beyond reasonable doubt. And that is how they get you in a violation of probation case.

The standard in a violation of probation case is "by a preponderance of the evidence." This means that it is more likely than not that you violated your probation. Now, when a person is on probation, they have to be sure that they maintain and comply with probation to avoid the violation. You can be found in violation for a number of reasons:

1. For a new arrest, which makes sense, but you don't have to be convicted of that new offense, you can be in violation and have your probation revoked based merely on the arrest.
2. For drug use. When on probation you must avoid using drugs because your probation officer can ask you for a urine sample at any time and you can be found in violation if they find any amount of drugs in your system.
3. For failure to comply with recommended substance abuse evaluation and treatment.
4. For failure to complete court-ordered community service.
5. For failure to report as requested by your probation officer.

If you are found in violation of your probation, you are exposed to the suspended period of incarceration. For example, if you were sentenced to two years of incarceration, execution suspended after two years of probation, and during that two year period you violate your probation, you may be sent to jail for anywhere up to that two year period. Violating probation is very serious, and there is one more thing you have to realize when it comes to probation violations - even with the burden being lower, even with the ease of violating you for even something minor, the state also gets the benefit of the fact that you are not entitled to a jury trial on a violation of probation. You only get a judge, and a judge will decide your fate. Now, when the judge handles a violation of probation, there are two main questions that need to be answered:

1. Did the defendant technically violate the probation? This is usually done by bringing in the probation officer or the police officer involved.
2. Is the purpose of probation no longer functioning - can the defendant no longer comply with probation such that jail is the only answer? Depending on your circumstance, there may be options below jail that have not been evaluated, so a criminal defense lawyer who handles a lot of these cases may have creative solutions.

No matter what you are facing, there are defenses that can be raised to a violation of probation, but only if you get a criminal defense lawyer involved.

Conclusion

Facing a criminal charge can be frightening and overwhelming. Hopefully, many of your basic questions about the criminal justice process have been answered in this book. If you still have questions, our office is happy to help. Simply contact Ruane Attorneys at 203-925-9200 to discuss your legal situation. We can provide additional resources and answer any questions that you may have. You do not have to go through a criminal case alone! We are here for you every step of the way.

Made in the USA
Monee, IL
04 November 2026

67379682R00056